EVERLASTING HARVEST

Art Director: Dana Irwin
Photography: Richard Babb
Production: Elaine Thompson, Dana Irwin

Library of Congress Cataloging-in-Publication Data
Dierks, Leslie.
    Everlasting harvest : making distinctive arrangements & elegant
decorations from nature / Leslie Dierks.
        p.   cm.
    "A Sterling/Lark book"
    Includes index.
    ISBN 0-8069-4866-3
    1. Dried flower arrangement.   I. Title.
SB449.3.D7D54   1995
745.92--dc20   95-38800
                                                                            CIP

10 9 8 7 6 5 4 3 2 1

A Sterling/Lark Book

Published by Sterling Publishing Co., Inc.
    387 Park Ave. South, New York, NY 10016

Created and produced by Altamont Press, Inc.
    50 College St., Asheville, NC 28801

© 1996, Altamont Press

Distributed in Canada by Sterling Publishing,
    c/o Canadian Manda Group, One Atlantic Avenue, Suite 105,
    Toronto, Ontario, Canada M6K 3E7
Distributed in Great Britain and Europe by Cassell PLC,
    Wellington House, 125 Strand, London, England WC2R 0BB
Distributed in Australia by Capricorn Link (Australia) Pty Ltd.,
    P.O. Box 6651, Baulkham Hills, Business Centre, NSW, Australia 2153

ISBN 0-8069-4866-3

EVERLASTING HARVEST

Making Distinctive Arrangements & Elegant Decorations from Nature

LESLIE DIERKS

Styling by Dana Irwin

Sterling Publishing Co., Inc. New York

A STERLING/LARK BOOK

26

84

48

132

95

114

78

contents

66

INTRODUCTION

Whatever your style of decoration, from country French to crisp modern, the presence of an artistic arrangement of natural materials adds warmth and color to your home. A garland draped gracefully over a door frame or a topiary placed on the mantel softens the hard geometry of the architecture. A floral centerpiece or a woodland wreath accents the color scheme of your furnishings.

Perhaps you've admired dried arrangements done by professionals, bought one from time to time, then wondered if you could make something similar yourself. If so, the answer is a resounding *yes!* The secret is not to be intimidated by the finished piece, but to plunge in and work one step at a time.

This book explores a wide variety of styles and methods for making natural arrangements. There are step-by-step instructions for eight of the most popular types of displays, from informal arrangements in containers to luxurious arches to hang on the wall. Each chapter includes more than a half-dozen design ideas to inspire you.

To make any of the projects in this book, you'll need only a few simple tools and some materials that you might gather from your own yard. If you prefer to purchase the ingredients for your arrangements, you'll find a wide assortment at craft shops, local farmers' markets, herb fairs, and even discount stores. Don't assume that you must have precisely the same materials you see in the photographs on these pages; one of the most satisfying aspects of floral design is adding your own special touch.

A single word of advice is offered to help you make the most of this book. When planning your display, consider the setting in which it will be placed before choosing the materials and style of arrangement. If you love roses and have your heart set on making a topiary, but the room is fairly casual in decor, consider making a topiary with a combination of roses and other flowers and foliage. Pink roses look less formal than red ones, and a terra-cotta pot makes a more casual container than a porcelain bowl.

Above all, relax and enjoy the process. Arranging natural materials is an art, not a science, and there are no right or wrong answers.

MATERIALS, TOOLS & BASIC TECHNIQUES

M aking your own distinctive arrangements requires nothing more than an assortment of attractive materials, the simplest of tools, and a little creativity. You'll find lots of exotic flowers and foliage at craft shops and floral supply houses, and native materials can be gathered from your own yard or nearby woods. The few tools required are readily available at craft stores and discount chains. And the creativity? It's right there at your fingertips.

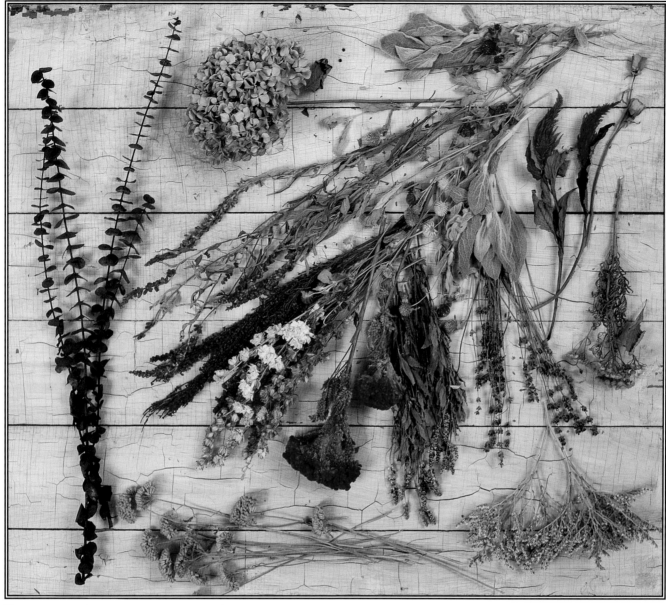

PICTURED HERE ARE JUST A FEW OF THE MANY DRIED HERBS AND FLOWERS YOU MIGHT CHOOSE FOR MAKING AN ARRANGEMENT.

Flowers and Herbs

Dried flowers and herbs are among the most popular materials used for making long-lasting wreaths, garlands, and arrangements in containers. Literally thousands of varieties exist, and you'll generally find a wide selection at florist shops, farmers' markets, herb farms, and craft supply stores. You may also enjoy drying your own flowers.

Collect flowers for drying just before their peak of bloom, since they continue to develop and may drop petals after cutting. Avoid picking blooms that are rain soaked or covered with dew; these may mold or develop blemishes. Because drying causes considerable shrinkage, gather more than you think you may need and cut each one with the longest possible stem.

Air drying is the simplest method, and it requires no special equipment. After removing most of the foliage, make small bunches of each type of plant and fasten the stems with rubber bands. As the stems contract, the rubber bands will continue to hold them together. Hang the plant clusters upside down in a dark, dry location that has good air circulation. Exposure to sunlight can fade the blossoms, and moist, stagnant air provides a haven for mold and mildew.

The amount of time needed to air dry flowers depends on their moisture content and the size of your bundles, but the process generally takes several days. Test a flower in the middle of one of your bunches; when you bend the stem it should snap easily.

For those who prefer more immediate results, a microwave oven can be used to dry plant materials quickly and effectively. Flowers and herbs can be dried in a brown paper bag or between a few paper towels, but this approach often results in a flattened appearance. A more certain method for maintaining a flower's full beauty is to surround it with particles of silica gel, a desiccant. (In fact, you can dry herbs and flowers in silica gel without a microwave, but they will need a couple of days to complete the process.)

Trim the stems of your materials to a length of about an inch (2.5 cm). Using a microwave-safe container, spread a layer of silica gel on the bottom, making it deep enough to hold the full length of the stems. Place the flowers so that they're not touching each other; then carefully sprinkle more crystals of silica gel inside and around the blossoms to cover them completely. Place the open container into your microwave and set the oven at the half-power or "defrost" level.

The amount of time varies according to type and number of materials, amount of silica gel, and model of oven; experiment with samples of your materials to see what times work best for you. Start with a brief amount, about 3 minutes, and add more time in short increments if needed. Keep in mind that anything baked in a microwave continues to cook after it has been removed. Allow several minutes of standing time for the process to complete itself.

Even if you don't plan to use it for all your materials, a microwave oven is very handy for drying leaves, moss, fungi, and pods. Leaves that merely crumble when air dried often dry very well by microwave. Moss, fungi, and other items collected from the wild frequently contain insects that can infest your projects and move into your home. Bake these in a paper bag or between paper towels at half power for 5 to 10 minutes.

Some arrangements can be made with fresh flowers that are subsequently allowed to dry in place. This is most successful when the type of arrangement allows you to use short stems; topiary forms and wreaths are two examples. Long stems tend to wilt as they dry, ruining the lines of your design. When making a fresh arrangement that you intend to let dry, place your materials closer together than you would ordinarily. Otherwise, the shrinkage from drying will leave unwelcome gaps.

WHEN ARRANGING FRESH FLOWERS TO DRY IN PLACE, PACK THE MATERIALS TIGHTLY TO ALLOW FOR SHRINKAGE.

Freeze drying is yet another method for preserving plant material. It's more successful than air drying for some delicate flowers, such as pansies, but it involves the use of very expensive equipment. Floral suppliers and some craft stores carry selected freeze-dried materials.

Foliage

Many people think foliage is ho-hum because they picture only the leatherleaf fern that invariably comes with the long-stemmed roses they purchase. In fact, the careful use of foliage can add just the right texture or bit of rich color needed to produce a dazzling composition.

When choosing foliage for your arrangements, be just as selective as you are with your flowers. Large-scale greenery, such as magnolia or palm leaves, is best used as a focal point to grab the eye or as a background against which other, smaller materials are placed. Smooth, pointed, medium-sized leaves make a striking contrast to rounded flower heads. When you're looking for texture or want to add more green color, consider plants with small or needlelike leaves.

Some kinds of foliage air dry very successfully—ivy and berried eucalyptus are two examples—but most become extremely brittle and crumble easily. The best alternative for these is preservation, a process that makes foliage feel smooth and supple. Many types of preserved greenery are available commercially, or you can make your own using a glycerine solution.

Add one part glycerine to two parts boiling water and mix thoroughly. After the solution has cooled to the touch, immerse the freshly cut stems. Be sure to remove any foliage below the level of the glycerine mixture.

Preserving leaves causes them to shift in color, and some darken considerably. You can dramatically change their hue by adding food dyes to your solution. The process can take from a few days to a few weeks to complete; you'll know that your foliage is ready when all of the leaves have altered in color.

WILD GRASSES, PODS, AND SEED HEADS COLLECTED FROM FIELDS AND FORESTS ADD IMMEASURABLY TO THE TEXTURAL VARIETY OF YOUR ARRANGEMENTS.

Pods, Lichens, Grasses, and Other Wild Things

A day spent outdoors collecting materials from the wild is lots more fun and often more productive than driving to a craft store. As your step slows from its everyday purposeful stride, your eyes will begin to notice the wealth of possibilities all around you.

In the woods you're likely to spot clumps of soft, green moss or unusual fungi growing in the moist shade. Fallen debris from

trees or the animals living in them might include abandoned nests, interesting nut casings, or beautiful, lichen-covered branches. Look for partially rotted root masses or gnarled vines that can add sculptural forms to your compositions.

Open areas abound in wild grasses, most of which dry extremely well. There you'll also find all sizes and types of seed heads and pods, which lend an air of the exotic to your creations. Seek out berry-producing plants such as bittersweet, holly, and viburnum.

As you're gathering wild materials for your projects, be mindful of your impact on the planet. Don't take all of what you see; leave enough of each plant so that it can return next year. No matter how tempting, never dig up a wild plant. Many have become endangered because of over-enthusiastic collectors.

Containers

An imaginative choice of containers can make even the most inexpensive collection of flowers look stunning. For those who don't happen to have an assortment of heirloom vases, there are lots of other possibilities close at hand. Scan your kitchen cabinets for interesting salad bowls, baking pans, crocks, and tumblers. If you're in the mood for buying something new, keep in mind that containers needn't be expensive to be beautiful. Antique-looking teapots, bowls, and vases are available for a pittance at flea markets, and import shops carry interesting baskets in many sizes, shapes, and colors.

When making your selection, decide what mood you want to create. A colorful floral arrangement placed in an antique earthenware pitcher would have an entirely different effect from that created by the same arrangement in a silver vase. Either one could be the right choice, depending upon the setting in which it's placed.

Relatively plain containers with interesting shapes are generally the most versatile. Those with highly patterned surfaces are more difficult because you must take the colors and designs into account when making your arrangement. In addition to the widely available and more conventional pottery vases, consider using containers made of wood, metal, glass, or stone.

RECOMMENDED TOOLS AND SUPPLIES (FROM BACK TO FRONT): WREATH BASES, GLUE GUN, POLYSTYRENE FOAM SPHERES AND CONES, SPOOL WIRE, STICKS OF HOT GLUE, WET FLORAL FOAM (DARK GREEN), DRY FLORAL FOAM (GRAY), PICKS, FLORAL PINS, FLORAL TAPE, "HAIRPINS" MADE OF FINE WIRE, AND WATERPROOF FLORAL TAPE.

Foam and Other Alternatives

Plastic foam is the most versatile and convenient substance to use inside a container to hold your plant materials in place. There are two basic types that you're likely to use, floral foam and polystyrene.

Floral foam comes in both wet and dry varieties. Wet floral foam, such as Oasis®, is most often used for fresh floral displays because it absorbs and holds water. It has a very fine consistency and tends to crumble easily, but some designers like to use it—without dampening it, of course—for dried materials because it accepts very delicate stems easily. Dry floral foam, such as Sahara®, is made to use with dried materials. It is similar to wet floral foam but is slightly firmer. Both types can be cut with a sharp knife into any shape desired.

Polystyrene is the least expensive type of foam and the strongest. It has a rougher texture than floral foam and tends to hold large stems and heavy materials more securely.

A less convenient alternative approach is to use sand and some wire mesh. Small stems glide readily into the sand, and the wire adds stability. The disadvantage to this approach is the mess created, especially when disassembling an arrangement later.

Wreath Bases

Ready-made bases for wreaths come in a variety of sizes, shapes, and materials and can be purchased at craft shops, garden supply stores, and even discount chains. Choose your base according to what look you want to achieve.

For a solid, full appearance, a straw wreath or polystyrene

base works well. Since these materials aren't attractive on their own, it's best to cover them completely with decorative materials.

Wire bases make wonderfully delicate wreaths, but these require that you add clusters of some type of background material. German statice and sweet Annie are two popular choices.

Bases made of vines or twigs are among the handsomest. They're often so attractive that many designers purposefully leave portions uncovered. Because they're made of natural materials, these bases offer the greatest variety, ranging in appearance from dainty to robust.

Floral Tape

The main purpose of floral tape is to disguise wires or unattractive stems. Available in green and brown, this thin, slightly elastic tape will adhere to itself when it's stretched and wrapped tightly.

A second variety of floral tape is waterproof and is used to secure pieces of floral foam into containers when you can't or don't want to use glue. This type of floral tape is dark green, very narrow, and quite adhesive.

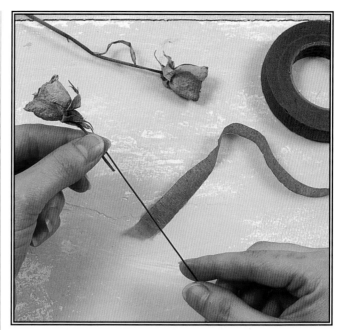

ADD LENGTH TO AN EXISTING STEM BY ATTACHING A STUB WIRE.

Floral Wire

Floral wire is just like normal wire except that it's painted green to be less obtrusive. It's available on spools and in precut lengths (stub wire) in a variety of gauges. Counter to instinct, a higher gauge number indicates a finer wire. For most dried materials, use wire that is fine enough to shape easily around the delicate stems. When wiring vines together or attaching bulky items, a heavier wire is the better choice.

Certain flowers, such as strawflowers, have hollow stems. These become so brittle when they dry that they almost always break off. Flower heads can be glued onto your arrangements, but if you need a stem, simply substitute a wire. Insert a stub wire through the flower head from the bottom, extending the wire far enough to form a small hook at the end. Pull the wire back into the flower to embed the hook firmly.

Stems that break or become too fragile during drying can be wired as well. Place a stub wire alongside the stem and attach the two together with floral tape. Starting near the bottom of the flower, set the tape on a diagonal and stretch it lightly as you wrap the flower and stem.

Short pieces of wire can be bent into U-shaped "hairpins" for attaching materials to foam when glue is less convenient or undesirable. Cut a piece about 3 inches (7.5 cm) long and bend it over your finger into a U.

FOR A FLOWER HEAD WITHOUT A STEM, A HOOK-SHAPED WIRE MAKES A GOOD SUBSTITUTE.

NEATLY FINISH YOUR PICKED CLUSTERS BY COVERING THEM WITH FLORAL TAPE.

Picks

Floral picks are essential tools for making most natural arrangements. They're very inexpensive, small pieces of wood, each with a sharp point at one end and a fine-gauge wire attached at the other. Picks are used to strengthen fragile stems or to bundle small clusters of materials together. When inserted into foam, they provide a secure means of attachment. Both regular and extra-long picks are available in green and natural wood.

To attach a small bundle of materials to a pick, start by breaking the stems to make them about half as long as the pick. Place the pick next to the bundle and wrap the wire two or three times around the stems. Then wrap the rest of the wire in a spiral down the stems and pick. The picked cluster can now be inserted into your foam base, but it will be much more secure if you wrap it first with floral tape.

Picks inserted at a slight angle, especially on a wreath base or in a swag, have better holding power. For hanging arrangements, you may want to apply some hot glue to the pick for added security.

Pins

Floral pins are similar to the U-shaped "hairpins" you can

make yourself, except that each one has a zigzag profile across the top. Also called fern pins and greening pins, these are most often used to attach Spanish moss and other delicate materials.

USE PLENTY OF HOT GLUE WHEN ATTACHING YOUR MATERIALS WITHOUT PICKS.

Glue Guns

Before glue guns were invented, every floral arrangement was constructed by picking, wiring, and pinning all the materials in place, a very time-consuming process. Hot glue not only reduces the time required, but it also increases your design possibilities.

Glue guns can be purchased in a variety of sizes and prices at craft shops, hardware stores, and discount centers. The glue is sold in opaque rods, but it becomes transparent when it melts and makes a nearly invisible bond. Both hot-melt and cool-melt guns and glue are available. Cool-melt glue is easier on your skin when you accidentally drip some, but its bond isn't as strong as the hot-melt variety.

When using a glue gun for the first time, many people make the mistake of applying too little glue to their materials. Clusters of flowers attached with skimpy amounts of glue tend to come apart and fall out of place. Be generous with the glue and make sure that all of the stems are covered.

One of the trademarks of an arrangement that has been assembled with a glue gun is the presence of fine, hairlike strands that look like spider webs. These catch the light and detract from the beauty of your work. A quick and easy way to eliminate them is to make a few brief passes over the arrangement with a hair dryer.

Caring for Your Arrangements

Although no arrangement lasts forever, you can extend the life of your projects by giving them the proper care and maintenance. By all means, never display your pieces where they will be exposed to direct sunlight. Even a brief dose of sunlight received on a daily basis is enough to age them prematurely. Flowers and foliage will become more fragile and tend to break easily, and their colors will fade to dull shades of brown and beige. Branches and vines will also become more brittle and may begin to lose their bark or outer coverings.

Both dried and preserved materials can absorb moisture from the air, and for that reason they should be displayed in areas where the humidity is lowest. Lingering moisture in the air can cause mold and mildew to develop on dried flowers and leaves. Preserved materials can actually "drip" dyed colored water if placed in a very humid environment. Unless it is very well ventilated, your bathroom is probably the least desirable location in the house for a long-term display of your favorite arrangement.

During its lifetime, which may be as long as several years, your display is likely to require cleaning. Accumulated dust and a few spider webs can rob a dried arrangement of its true color and beauty. If your piece is made of driftwood, moss, and berries, a light going-over with a feather duster may be sufficient. For a more delicate floral display, the best approach is to use a hair dryer. Use the cold setting and avoid prolonged concentration in a single area. A soft, natural-bristle artist's brush is helpful for removing stubborn dust particles.

Whenever you take time to clean it, inspect your arrangement for broken stems and materials that no longer look their best. Now is the perfect time to freshen it up by adding a few new materials.

A CONTORTED BRANCH, SUCH AS THIS HAWTHORN, MAY INSPIRE YOU TO CREATE A DRAMATIC SCULPTURAL ARRANGEMENT.

AN ARRANGEMENT OF NATURAL MATERIALS ADDS A SPECIAL TOUCH TO ANY ROOM

INFORMAL ARRANGEMENTS

Informal arrangements
are just that—casual and
inexact in the placement
and choice of each material.
This doesn't mean that
they're unplanned. Even
the most casual grouping of
materials should be assembled with thought given to
color, texture, and scale.
The most successful informal arrangements are those
that appear natural; even
though all your materials
don't naturally grow in the
same location, they should
blend well together.

1.

Once you've selected your container, fill it with floral foam. There's no need to cut a single large block to the exact shape; it's easier to glue a few smaller pieces together, and a few gaps between the pieces of foam won't affect your arrangement. If you're making a permanent arrangement or using an inexpensive cardboard liner, secure your foam with hot glue. Otherwise, tape your foam into the container to hold it steady.

2.

Cut a piece of sheet moss to cover your foam and tuck it in around the edges of the container.

3.

Pick clusters of greenery, using floral tape to cover the wires on the picks. Sweet Annie is shown here; it was chosen for its delicate texture and light green color. Ferns or evergreens would be less subtle but would work equally well.

4.

Place your focal-point flowers—in this case, large hydrangea blossoms. Single woody stems can be inserted directly into the foam without the need for picking.

5.

Establish the overall dimensions of your arrangement with the longest stems of flowers and greenery. Then gradually fill in the shape you desire. In an arrangement that will be placed on a shelf or mantel, you will most likely want the taller materials in back and shorter ones in front. Remember to fill evenly all around; even those pieces placed near a wall may be viewed from either side, and gaps in your arrangement make it look unfinished.

6.

Your last step is to insert the most fragile elements, such as roses and peonies, which might be damaged by frequent handling.

MAKING AN INFORMAL ARRANGEMENT

DESIGN

Josena McCaig

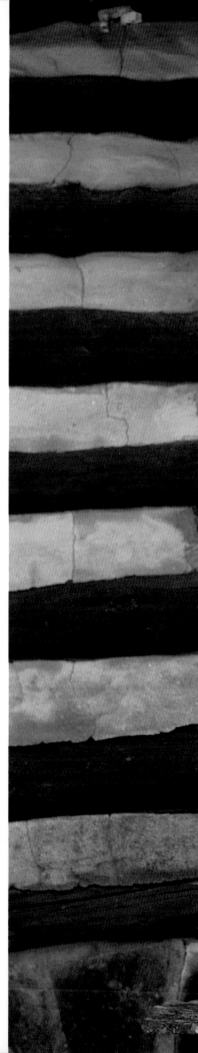

A tobacco-gathering basket, with its wide slats and open weave, makes a striking background for this impressive arrangement. Such baskets can be found in antique shops and some floral supply stores.

The arrangement itself is notable for its airiness, despite the solidity of many of its ingredients. The secret is not to pack the elements too closely together. Allow each one enough space to retain its identity.

Wire a block of foam onto the base and cover it with sheet moss. Then begin to establish the shape you want by placing a few of your largest materials. Here three banksias (a type of protea) form a triangle within the larger triangular shape of the arrangement. The mahogany, badam nut, and other pods carry the composition to the edges of the basket and just beyond. Extend the lines farther with a few twisted green fronds of dried coco lashing, some pieces of curly willow, and a few grasses such as setaria. Fill in as needed with clusters of caspia.

DESIGN

◆

Bill Parker

When selecting a container for your arrangement, your eye might easily pass over such a plain alternative as this simple wicker basket. In fact, decorating the rim is a splendid alternative to placing flowers into a basket, and for this purpose a plain weave is often the best choice.

Begin by gluing tips of bracken fern all around the rim, covering both the inside and outside edges. Cut the stems from about a dozen open, freeze-dried roses and glue the flower heads in clusters of two or three around the rim. Add peonies and small bunches of rose buds near the open roses. Then cut the tips from preserved olive branches and glue them around each grouping of flowers and into the open spaces. Attach clusters of small roses onto the leaves and fill any remaining spaces with bundles of purple oregano and lavender. Cover any visible glue with bits of moss. If desired, attach a bow made of French wired ribbon to the handle.

DESIGN
◆
Josena McCaig

When planning your arrangements, cast your eye about for unusual items that might be used as containers. Decorative objects, such as these bird-houses made of weathered barn boards and rustic metal roofing, can stimulate lots of ideas for designs that are a bit out of the ordinary.

Wherever you want to add touches of floral color, first glue on a dab of sheet moss and a few sprigs of German statice. Then attach short stems of the flowers and other materials of your choice. These arrangements feature hydrangea florets, small pieces of pink and lavender larkspur, roses, artichokes, cockscomb, globe amaranth, ixodia daisies, and strawflowers. After the flowers are all in place, glue lacy bits of lichen moss into corners and onto edges to soften the hard lines of the wooden structures.

DESIGN

◆

Jane Dicus

Mixing wild materials with exotic ones can produce fabulous effects, especially when you use a container that's as interesting as this turtle pot. When you're out collecting wildflowers and grasses, look for those with unusual shapes or textures to add to your composition.

To make an arrangement similar to this one, start by filling your container with polystyrene foam. Make sure the foam extends above the lip of your basket or bowl so that you can insert some of the stems at lower angles.

Insert a strong vertical element first; the one used here is a decorative banana stick. Then place your focal-point flowers—pincushion proteas and leucodendron. Cluster the filler material, placing the wild grasses all on the right and the iris pods and okra pods on the left.

DESIGN

◆

Cynthia
Gillooly

This lush floral arrangement is literally a drawerful; the long, narrow container is actually a drawer from an old treadle sewing machine. The curved edge of the drawer adds a graceful line to the front of the arrangement, and the less interesting straight edge faces toward the back.

After filling the container with floral foam, insert clusters of German statice as a low background for your other flowers. Set the height of the arrangement along the back of the container with stems of pink and lavender larkspur and green oregano inserted into the foam. Making a loose, random arrangement of colors and textures, fill in the rest of the container with annual statice, strawflowers, globe amaranth, hydrangea, roses, ixodia daisies, and green amaranth. Vary the height of the stems to give your composition greater depth and interest. As a final touch, insert an individual jade or bay leaf wherever a green accent is needed.

DESIGN

◆

Jane Dicus

32

There are two ways to add drama to your arrangement: build a tightly controlled design or incorporate some unusual materials. This is a fairly casual design, but it includes papyrus, badam nut pods, and peacock feathers. The container is an imported basket made of roots and vines. If your local craft shops don't carry materials identical to these, substitute others that have interesting shapes and textures.

To make this arrangement, place a block of floral foam into your container and cover it with sheet moss. Start with the tallest papyrus spike to set the height; then place the other two to form a gentle curve when viewed from the front. If desired, hot-glue a small pine needle bird's nest to the right of this curve. Then add a few badam nut pods and several small clusters of purple delphinium and nigella. Wire and pick all of the heavy or thick stems and cover the wire with floral tape. To complete the arrangement, embellish it with peacock feathers and one or two slender curving branches; then add a small bird to the nest.

DESIGN

◆

Bill Parker

WREATHS

Wreaths are among the most popular of natural arrangements and are very easy to make. Interesting bases in a variety of sizes and shapes are readily available, or you can construct your own from lengths of heavy wire or vines. Although circular wreaths are the most common, it's fun to experiment with hearts, ovals, and squares.

DESIGN

◆

J o s e n a   M c C a i g

1.

Begin with the wreath base of your choice. A vine base is versatile because it's sturdy, materials can be easily glued to it, and portions of the vine can be left undecorated to form an asymmetrical design. Before adding your materials, make a hanger by attaching a loop of sturdy wire to the back.

2.

For a wreath where the entire surface is covered, begin by choosing a background material. This design calls for sweet Annie; a totally different effect would result from substituting German statice or preserved cedar.

3.

After making a small cluster, apply hot glue to the stems. Be generous with the glue; otherwise your materials may work loose with time. Work around the wreath, applying each succeeding cluster so that its foliage covers the stems of the prior one.

4.

There are as many different ways to style your wreath as there are designers. This wreath employs a technique called clustering. Gather stems of blue larkspur into small bunches and glue them into several locations around the wreath. Then repeat with clusters of bright yellow sanfordi.

5.

Break off small pieces of preserved cedar–or any other contrasting material–and place them evenly around the inner and outer edges of the wreath. This type of coverage will ensure that your wreath looks equally beautiful when viewed from the side.

6.

Finally, attach your focal-point flowers. Here two to three miniature sunflowers are grouped together and glued onto selected locations around the wreath. Cover any exposed glue with small bits of moss.

Some wreath bases are so handsome that they can—and should—be left partially uncovered to become part of the overall design. Here the color and texture of birch bark perfectly complement the other ingredients in a woodsy wreath.

The hardness and beauty of the bark pose a challenge for attaching materials; it's very difficult to insert picks through the bark, and it seems a pity to use hot glue on such fine material. Instead, wire a block of floral foam to the base and cover the foam with sheet moss.

To begin your decoration, insert three stemmed artichokes into the foam, creating an asymmetrical triangle. Then reinforce that general shape with dried sunflowers and clusters of dudinea. Fill in with sprigs of caspia and clusters of white berries. If desired, glue bits of moss and small pieces of lichen to the wreath base for added texture.

DESIGN

◆

Bill Parker

dainty floral coronet is the perfect accessory to wear for a special springtime occasion. It's equally easy to make from dried materials or from fresh flowers that will dry in place.

Start with a single crimped-wire wreath base or with 20 to 23 inches (51 to 58.5 cm) of 18-gauge wire formed into a ring. Beginning in one place and moving around the ring, attach small clusters of a preserved evergreen such as princess pine. Use floral tape to make the attachment, and overlap the clusters so that the foliage hides the tape. Then hot-glue a loose circlet of raffia and a looped ribbon onto the wreath at about five or six places. Glue sprigs of heather at several locations, with some facing outward and others inward toward the center hole. Onto this colorful background, glue roses, bells-of-Ireland, annual statice, baby's-breath, and tips of seeded eucalyptus. If desired, add a bow to match the ribbon.

DESIGN

✦

Janet Frye

When making your own wreaths, don't limit yourself to circular bases. Square-, oval-, and heart-shaped wreaths offer lots of design possibilities, and customized bases are easy to build yourself.

To create a romantic-looking wreath like this one, begin with about 4 feet (1.2 m) of galvanized clothesline wire. Form the wire into a square using a pair of pliers, measuring to confirm that your sides are equal in length. Overlap the ends and cut off the excess; then fasten the wire together with duct tape. Finally, cover the entire base with floral tape.

Make mixed bunches of blue and white larkspur, artemisia, sweet Annie, globe thistle, setaria, and sago. Wire the bunches together and tape the ends. Then tape the bunches to the base, working them all in the same direction around the square. In the spaces between clusters, glue white carnations and full-size and miniature poppy pods, making clusters of the minipods. Create a focal point by gluing or wiring an interesting branch into one corner; just lift the material and attach it to the base. Carry through this theme by gluing small pieces of root or vine into the opposite corner. As a final garnish, glue one perfect banksia blossom where the branch attaches to the wreath.

DESIGN
◆
Diane Weaver

Rich in color and texture, this autumnal wreath speaks of grain-filled silos, rows of sky-high sun- flowers, and fields of wild- flowers. Its base is a wire ring, which enables you to make a wreath that is deli- cate and airy in appearance as well as light in weight.

Start with a wire ring in the desired size—this one is 12 inches (30.5 cm) in diame- ter—and wrap it with floral tape. Before adding any flowers, make a hanger by forming a piece of wire or chenille stem into a loop and fastening it directly to the wreath base.

Working around the ring in a single direction, attach small bunches of German statice. Wire each bunch together and use the end of the wire to attach the bunch to the base. As you add each new bunch, cover the stems and exposed wire on the pre- vious one. Insert individual stems of oats, wheat, and foxtail grass every few inch- es to provide texture and dimension. Hot-glue orange marigolds, sunflowers, and blue globe thistles around the wreath for bright dabs of color. Fill in with orange strawflowers and sweet Annie. Finally, add touches of blue larkspur for depth and short pieces of bitter- sweet for texture.

DESIGN

◆

Barbara Applebaum

Twig bases make especially handsome wreaths; they're bulky enough to provide some substance, yet their open construction allows the finished piece to look delicate and airy. These bases also provide plenty of surfaces to which you can glue your materials.

Begin by hot-gluing individual orange safflowers (with their foliage) onto several locations around the wreath. Moving around the circle in a single direction, add small bunches of hydrangea, purple annual statice, and ixodia daisies. Fill in any gaps with clusters of tansies, jade leaves, and sago. Tuck in bits of lichen moss around the wreath for added texture.

DESIGN

◆

Jane Dicus

The first step in making a "wild" wreath is often the most fun—taking a walk in the woods to collect interesting materials. This wreath includes mosses, fungi, lichens, cones, branches, pods, feathers, and even an abandoned hummingbird's nest. For added interest, it also has a looped braid made from the sheaths of a split philodendron plant.

A sheath is produced each time this plant grows a new leaf. As the leaf emerges, the sheath becomes dry and brittle and falls off. Soak three sheaths in hot water for about an hour; then braid them together, leaving the leafy ends free. Insert the braid into a space in the vine base, make a loop, and hot-glue it in place.

This wreath uses a purchased base that's made of a vine native to the Philippines, but you could easily substitute any vine base. Using the materials you've collected, glue clumps of similar mosses onto the base in three locations to form a rough triangle. Glue a few thin, pliable branches to the lower left; then spiral them around the wreath and glue them again near the top center. Now add fungi, lichens, and other woodsy treasures around the wreath, using the shape of the vine to guide your placement.

Make a small vertical arrangement of materials on the right side, starting with a handful of curly willow branches. Add pinecones, sumac, thistles, and a cluster of pussy willow, all pointing upwards. Finish the wreath by adding a few selected feathers.

DESIGN
◆
Patti Hill

An oval base makes a subtle but noticeable difference in the appearance of a wreath. The shape seems a bit old-fashioned—it is reminiscent of old photographs—and it works especially well with combinations of flowers that were popular during the Victorian era.

For a simple and inexpensive wreath base, use an oval basket hoop. Cover it with bundles of juniper tips glued all around, facing some pieces in toward the center and some outward. Break a few large heads of cockscomb and hydrangea into pieces about 3 inches (7.5 cm) across. Make bundles of two or three pieces and attach them in various locations around the wreath. Make small bunches of roses, with their leaves, and place them in areas between the larger blossoms. Now add a few clusters of burgundy-dyed and preserved salal leaves. Finally, fill in with heather and koala ladder and cover any exposed glue with bits of sheet moss.

DESIGN

◆

Josena McCaig

TOPIARY FORMS

topiaries are trees or shrubs that have been trimmed, often over a period of years, into decorative shapes that range from classical geometric forms to whimsical animals and interesting objects. With dried and preserved materials, it's easy to produce similar topiary designs. Many are designed to have a main stem or trunk to mimic the appearance of a living topiary.

DESIGN

◆

Cynthia Gillooly

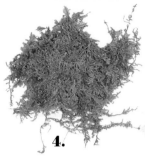

1.

Choose a branch substantial enough to suit the size of your topiary ball, keeping in mind that the materials you add will increase the final size. This piece, when complete, has a ball diameter of about 6 inches (15 cm) and the stem measures about 1 inch (2.5 cm) thick. Then cut both ends of the branch into a dull point.

2.

Firmly glue polystyrene foam into a terra-cotta pot. Topiaries tend to be top heavy and should be well secured at the base. (When making a large, floor-size topiary, fill your container with plaster of Paris or florist's clay; foam and hot glue are sufficient for tabletop projects.) Then insert the branch well into the foam and anchor it with hot glue.

3.

Cover the foam in the pot with sheet moss and glue it in place.

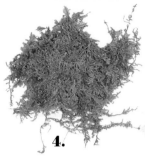

4.

Then poke the top end of the branch into a polystyrene sphere, inserting the branch about three-quarters of the way into the ball. Secure the branch into the foam with hot glue.

5.

Using three or four different kinds of moss, glue small pieces onto the foam sphere. Vary the arrangement of mosses as you work your way around the ball to create a rich tapestry of textures and colors.

6.

Finish by gluing small lichens onto the branch and placing a sponge mushroom into the moss at the base.

two-tiered topiary is no more difficult to make than a more common single one, and it offers plenty of design options. If a double-balled topiary form isn't readily available, make your own using a wooden dowel and two polystyrene foam spheres. This one requires a 3/4-inch-diameter (2-cm) wooden dowel about 18 inches (45.5 cm) long and two foam balls, 4 inches (10 cm) and 6 inches (15 cm) in diameter.

After inserting the dowel into the polystyrene foam in your container, place the spheres at the desired heights on the dowel. Use glue to hold the balls in place and to secure the dowel at the base. Then cover the exposed dowel with green floral tape and bits of sheet moss.

When covering the curved surfaces of the balls with sheet moss, dampen the moss to make it easier to manipulate without tearing. Attach the moss to the foam with short "hairpins" made of 22-gauge wire. To make a hairpin, just bend a short length of wire into a U and insert it through the moss. (Glue forms a barrier and makes it more difficult to insert delicate flower stems later.)

Embellish the topiary with a swirl of honeysuckle vine; insert one end into the base and make a spiral up the form, securing it where necessary with wire hairpins. Begin the colorful floral spiral that decorates the double form by attaching clusters of pepperberries, complete with their leaves, strawflowers, and heather. It's easiest to make a graceful curve if you start with a sparse line of color and gradually thicken it. Add yellow button chrysanthemums and touches of moss and lichen for highlights, attaching them with glue and/or hairpins.

DESIGN

◆

Janet Frye

Often topiaries are designed to bring a bit of amusement or wonder to those who view them. These spheres are an unorthodox combination of a natural material with something man-made. Upholstery tacks are the only means used to hold these eucalyptus leaves in place, which allows the edges of the leaves to curl open as they dry. This gives each sphere a unique and interesting silhouette.

Start with three or four packages of upholstery tacks, several stems of berried eucalyptus, and three polystyrene foam balls. These balls are 5, 4, and 2-1/2 inches (12.5, 10, and 6.5 cm) in diameter, but you can make them just about any size.

Be sure to use fresh eucalyptus leaves, which are moist and pliable. If you allow them to dry first, they will break easily and won't conform to the shape of your sphere. Starting at the top, secure one end of a leaf with a tack. Place another leaf slightly overlapping the first and hold the two together with another tack.

Continue overlapping leaves roughly in rows until the sphere is completely covered. The variation in size and shape of the leaves adds interest to the placement of your tacks, preventing them from becoming too regular.

DESIGN

◆

Cynthia Gillooly

This traditional floral top-iary is perfect for nearly any room of the house. Its relatively small scale—only about 12 inches (30.5 cm) in height—allows it to fit easily on a dressing table, at your writing desk, or on a mantel.

As you can see on page 11, this topiary was constructed with fresh materials that were allowed to dry in place. If you make yours this way, be sure to pack in more filler flowers than you think you need. The roses will shrink substantially as they dry.

After securing a base of polystyrene foam into your container, make a stem using three or four curly willow branches wired together at the top and bottom. Then insert the stem into the foam, gluing it in place, and cover the foam with sheet moss.

For the topiary, place a ball of wet floral foam onto the stem and hot-glue it in place. Then thoroughly soak the foam. Insert fresh sweetheart roses, scattering them across the surface of the ball. Add bits of fresh heather and caspia, seed clusters from seeded eucalyptus, and small touches of baby's-breath and baronia heather.

You can keep your topiary fresh for a week or more by misting at least once per day. When it starts to fade, dry it quickly in a warm, dark location.

Other flowers that are easily dried in place are German statice, annual statice, button chrysanthemums, and yarrow.

DESIGN

◆

Janet Frye

65

Sleek and contemporary, this topiary employs a restricted palette to accentuate its textural variety and overall composition. Its unusual egg shape reflects a tradition well established in the topiary arts for making highly creative and sometimes whimsical forms.

After placing polystyrene foam into your container, make a stem for the topiary. To keep within the range of greens desired, this one consists of about 10 to 15 rose stems wired together at the top and bottom, but other woody stems or small branches would work equally well. When complete, insert the stem into the foam and secure it with hot glue.

To make the topiary, cut a block of floral foam into an egg shape and make a hole in the bottom for the stem. Glue individual leaves of silver dollar eucalyptus onto the egg, starting at the top. Slightly overlap the edges of the leaves and create a bricklike pattern with the rows; i.e., offset the leaves so that the seams aren't perfectly aligned.

When the egg is completely covered, mount it on the stem and secure it with glue.

Embellish the topiary with bells-of-Ireland, making a collar around the bottom and a small cluster at the top. Then spray the piece with a clear acrylic coating. Glue a few stems of bear grass around the base where the stem joins the foam. Finally, cover the foam with sheet moss and place a few selected river rocks at the base.

DESIGN

◆

Janet Frye

Not all arrangements must be large to be effective; a miniature topiary garden beckons the eye and draws the viewer closer to investigate its mysteries. This one features a collection of mosses, and you can create a totally different design just by using flowers instead. Although the components are grouped closely together to make the garden, they remain detached and can be used individually as well.

Make each topiary by inserting a branch into a 3-inch (7.5-cm) foam ball. Insert the other end of the branch into a container filled with polystyrene foam. To keep the topiary in scale, use a container only about 1/2 inch (1.5 cm) larger in width than the diameter of your foam ball. Glue the joints between the branch and the foam for stability.

Begin gluing four or five types of dried mosses and lichens to the ball, starting at the top. Work your way around to cover the surface evenly and to create a random pattern. After the ball is completely covered, glue some mosses and lichens onto the base. Finish each topiary by winding some bittersweet or honeysuckle vine around the base of the trunk for decoration.

To make the garden space between the topiaries, bunch several clumps of dried moss into a small flat tray, using dabs of hot glue as needed to hold the mosses together. Glue a few lichens on top for added interest.

DESIGN

◆

Anne Cook

This mysterious-looking topiary is covered entirely with the flat, somewhat translucent seedpods of *Lunaria*, which is more commonly known as money plant. Unlike many topiaries, this one sits directly on its base without a stem. The result looks similar to a reflecting ball in a garden.

Starting at the top and working down, glue individual seedpods to a white polystyrene ball. Use cool-melt glue or rubber cement rather than hot-melt glue to give yourself sufficient time to place each pod where desired. To get complete coverage, slightly overlap the pods. When the ball is evenly covered, hot-glue it to a wooden pedestal whose top surface has been covered with metallic ribbon. Finish the arrangement with a skirt of seedpods where the ball meets the wooden base.

DESIGN

◆

Janet Frye

Live topiaries have traditionally taken on fanciful shapes that were limited only by the imaginations of their creators. This magnificent floral cake and its accompanying tablecloth of galax leaves are fine expressions of that tradition. In combination they make a stunning display for a birthday party; the cake alone would be an impressive Mother's Day gift.

Like any good cake, this one is made in layers. Cut a thick sheet of polystyrene foam into three 8-inch (20.5-cm) rounds and hot-glue the rounds together to make a cake. Then cut out a wedge. Place a ribbon around the center of the cake and glue it into place. Brush some water-based, clear-drying glue onto the top of the cake and sprinkle the tacky surface with lavender potpourri. When this has dried, begin attaching the larger flowers such as roses, dogwood, pansies, and individual seedpods from a money plant. Apply a small amount of hot glue to each stem and press the flower into place. Start at the top; then glue flowers

around the sides of the cake. Fill in around the larger blossoms with larkspur and miniature rose buds.

To make a galax tablecloth, use preserved leaves (they're much more supple than dried ones) and a piece of felt cut to the desired size. Starting in the middle of the felt, attach one leaf to the felt with a small amount of hot glue. Apply the next leaf by overlapping the first and gluing it into place. Work your way around the felt, positioning leaves in a circular pattern.

DESIGN

◆

Anne Cook

ARCHES, SWAGS & GARLANDS

arches, swags, and garlands are ideal for decorating difficult areas, where container arrangements or wreaths just won't work. They're also well suited for embellishing large pieces of furniture, such as the head of a bed or a corner china cabinet. Garlands can be constructed as long or short as you wish, and you can customize the size and shape of an arch or swag to fit perfectly into an empty space.

MAKING AN ARCH

DESIGN

◆

Josena McCaig

1.

Arches and swags can be made using a variety of bases; for one that's full and lush, choose a solid base made of vines or straw. One easy way to make your own is to cut a section from a grapevine wreath base. Secure the vines by firmly wrapping the entire length with spool wire. Then attach a loop of sturdy wire at the center to use when hanging the arch.

2.

On each end, hot-glue clusters of your background material so that the foliage, not the stems, overextends the tips of the vines. Preserved olive is used here for its pale grey-green color.

3.

Build out the center portion of the arch—it should be more three-dimensional than the ends—and begin to add your focal points. Lift the olive leaves to glue on the chile peppers and insert some of them facing outward in the center of the arch.

4.

To attach the garlic clusters, make a loop with the braided stems and apply a generous amount of glue to the back of the loop.

5.

As you fill in with smaller materials, turn the piece and view it from the top to make sure that you don't leave any gaps or areas lacking color.

MAKING A GARLAND

DESIGN
◆
Josena McCaig

1.

The base of a garland must be flexible so that it can drape naturally when you hang it, and the size of the wire needed depends on the weight of your materials. For a heavy culinary garland like this one, electrical wire or a similar heavy wire is recommended. It's rugged yet easily bent into the desired shape during installation. Cover the entire length of the wire with floral tape.

2.

Further hide the wire by surrounding it with Spanish moss. Use spool wire to wrap the moss in place.

3.

Periodically along the length of the garland, attach your focal-point materials with hot glue. To coordinate with its companion arch, this garland includes clusters of sunflowers, tansy, safflower, artemisia, and garlic. As you did on the arch, form the braided garlic stems into a loop and glue the arrangement onto the garland.

4.

Fill in the bulk of the garland by gluing on smaller flowers and stems of preserved olive to match the color and texture of the arch

Nothing speaks of the harvest season more effectively than golden grains and brilliant yellow sunflowers. This simple arch, which abounds with grasses, berries, pods, and wildflowers, will brighten up your home throughout many changes of season.

It's made of curly willow and other tree branches bunched together in the middle and held with wire. To provide a means for attaching the other materials, hot-glue a piece of floral foam in the center of the branches. After covering the foam with moss, begin inserting individual sunflowers so that they radiate outward. Use longer stems for the sides and shorter ones for top and bottom. Add clusters of rye, wheat, and oats at various lengths and angles, followed by stems of rose hips, bittersweet, and canella berries. Fill in with pussy willow, nigella, sweet rocket, yarrow, santolina, blackeyed Susans, and a variety of pods. Insert a few branches of untreated eucalyptus on either side to provide some greenery. Finally, hot-glue a few fungi and a hornet's nest in the center.

DESIGN

Barbara Applebaum

The pleasing curves of this swag are formed by a serpentine grapevine base. Such bases can be purchased ready-made or you can construct your own from pieces of vine wired together. To reproduce the delicate quality of this swag, be sure to include several fine, curly tendrils of vine on the ends.

Starting in the center and moving outward, hot-glue small bunches of German statice to the vine. As you move toward the ends, space the clusters slightly farther apart to create an airy appearance. Now add your main flowers and grains—Queen Anne's lace, white yarrow, and black beard wheat—by gluing them directly to the vine. Cluster the flowers in the center of the swag and angle them so that they radiate outward. Fill in any holes between the larger materials with pink delphinium; then place a few stems of delphinium on either end, angling them to show nicely against the shape of the vine base.

DESIGN

◆

Bill Parker

A bundle of moss- and lichen-covered birch twigs provides the structure for a delightful spring arrangement. Long pieces are wired and glued together into an arch, and shorter twigs are attached to add dimension and texture to the form.

Establish a framework for the flowers by gluing stems of jade and bay leaves to the base. Then place three hydrangea stems in a rough triangle near the center. Fill in the central focal point with burgundy larkspur and roses, pale lavender larkspur, and bundles of ixodia daisies. Insert a pitcher plant on each end and add clusters of larkspur, ixodia daisies, and santolina on each side to carry the color outward from the center.

DESIGN

◆

J a n e   D i c u s

Floral garlands are easy to construct, and they add a wonderful line of color to the top of a cabinet, along a mantel, or over a bed. Choose flowers and a ribbon that will harmonize with the furnishings of your room.

This garland is very lightweight and flexible because its base is a single strand of 18- or 20-gauge wire. Cut a length of spool wire a little longer than you would like your garland to be; this allows you to construct a small loop at each end to make installation easier. After securing the wire at both ends to hold it steady, fill in the bulk of the base with small bunches of German statice. Wire clusters of the flowers together and tape the ends of the stems. Then tape the bunches to the wire base so that the flowers in each cluster conceal the stems of the previous one.

Begin your embellishment by looping and tying several strands of raffia to the floral base. Then wire a patterned ribbon intermittently along the length of the garland. Glue on some rose-colored annual statice, miniholly, and globe amaranth. For added texture, include a few gilded iris pods and some berried eucalyptus. Finish with a small hornet's nest glued near the center.

DESIGN
◆
Cynthia
Gillooly

The mixture of wild and exotic ingredients in this arch produces an elegant and impressive result. The use of a brocade ribbon as one of the focal points adds a touch of formality and serves to highlight the deep red natural elements.

To give the arch an open and airy appearance, use a rectangular block of polystyrene foam as the base. Then, before adding anything to the foam, make a sturdy hanger. Insert a piece of wire through the foam and bend up both ends. Position a wooden pick between the wire and foam on each side and glue the two picks in place. Then twist the wire into a loop. The picks will prevent the wire hanger from pulling through the foam.

After covering the base with sheet moss, create the outline of your arch with branches of manzanita. Then make your central focal point with a brocade ribbon bow and two leucodendron blossoms. Add a palm frond on either side and place small clusters of proteas into the open areas. Insert sumac pods, stems of red-dyed silver dollar eucalyptus, and purple annual statice wherever bursts of bright color are needed. Finally, add linear elements such as a stem of buriti fruit, four or five pieces of assegai (the curled, tubular stems), and some sparkled ting-ting.

DESIGN
◆
Jamie McCabe

Arrangements made with evergreens are most common during the holiday season, but they make equally dramatic accents all year round. To avoid a design that looks like an untimely Christmas decoration, choose broad-leaved evergreens and cedar rather than fir and pine as your main ingredients.

Begin this arch by cutting a 36-inch (91.5-cm) plastic-covered straw wreath base into two halves and covering the cut ends with wide plastic tape to hold the straw in place. Set aside one half for another project. A piece this large is quite heavy, so make a wire hanger at each end of the arch with 18-gauge wire. Then cover the entire piece with sheet moss to hide the plastic and provide a base for gluing smaller fill-in pieces later.

Working from the ends toward the center, begin picking pieces of preserved green cedar and placing them in an overlapping position, with the greenery of the each piece hiding the pick from the last. Add depth to your work by arranging the pieces at different angles and varying the length of the materials. Fill in the center area of the arch with preserved magnolia and add accents of fern, green ivy (with berries), Australian miniholly, and a few wispy grasses. Place a few of the magnolia leaves into the cedar on the ends and use the finer materials to soften the outline and create a more open and natural look.

DESIGN

◆

Cathy Barnhardt

STRUCTURED ARRANGEMENTS

Structured arrangements are formal not in the sense that they are to be used for ceremonial occasions but that their assembly is organized to produce a specific result. An arrangement with a clear structure is especially pleasing because the eye is guided to rest in turn upon each component. Whether you choose a classic design, such as the Biedermeier style or Hogarth curve, or create one of your own, be sure that the structural elements come together into a balanced composition.

MAKING A STRUCTURED ARRANGEMENT

DESIGN

Josena McCaig

1.

A tiered arrangement is one of the easiest structures to accomplish. Begin with a long, narrow container filled with floral foam. If you use a basket, wire the foam through the bottom of the basket to secure it.

2.

Cut a piece of sheet moss to fit over the foam and tuck it in around the edges of the container.

3.

Place a row of materials down the middle of your container. (Note: Some designers prefer to start with the back row and move forward; try both approaches and decide which feels most comfortable to you.)

4.

If you use small clusters (tapestry millet is shown here), pick the materials; otherwise insert single stems directly into the foam.

5.

Place a row of a slightly taller material behind the middle row. The material in front should obscure the stems, not the flower heads, of the material behind.

6.

Continue building backward, making each layer somewhat taller than the one before it. Fan some of the materials outward to make the arrangement look full and lush.

7.

Begin adding rows of materials in front of the middle, stepping down in height as you move forward. Vary the textures and colors for visual interest. Here the smooth skin of the pitcher plants and poppy pods contrasts well with the fine-textured rice grass and sweet Annie.

8.

When you reach the very front of your container, use materials with short, curving stems, such as these pieces of preserved cedar and clusters of canella berries. Place these so that they arc outward and down over the lip of the container.

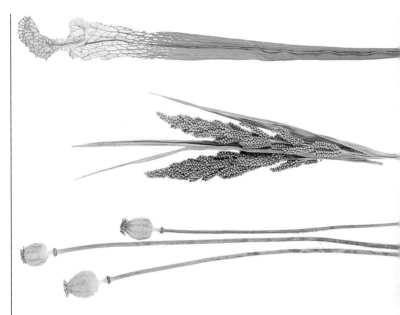

Hot summer days spent strolling along a riverbank are brought to mind by this impressive arrangement. It's built in a simple clay saucer that has been "weathered" with a splattering of moss green and brown paints.

Fill a 12-inch (28.5-cm) clay saucer with polystyrene foam and secure the foam in place with hot glue. Trim the stems on two bunches of pencil cattails to the desired length, saving the trimmings. Then insert the cattails into the foam to form a thick row across the back of the container. If the cattails don't look dense enough on their own, back them with a narrow row of a more solid dried material, such as lemon-leaf eucalyptus.

Make a second row with eight palm leaves, each cut to a wide point. Slightly overlap the palms and leave small spaces between those in front. Fill the space on the right and create a crescent-shaped white mass with clusters of Australian daisies. Graduate the height of the clusters, starting with the tallest stems in the back.

Using the reserved cattail stems, make small clusters held together at the bottoms with rubber bands. Cut them across the tops to make smooth bevels; then hot-glue the stem clusters to the foam. Now fill in the spaces around the stems with small bunches of lavender inserted into the foam.

Glue three lotus pods to the front of the saucer by first carving out a space on the back of each of the bottom two pods to fit onto the lip of the container. Complement the pods with a natural-looking mushroom bird glued to their left. Finish with bits of lichen glued onto the edges and bits of moss tucked in wherever the foam shows.

DESIGN

◆

Janet Frye

The casualness of a hollowed-out log container contrasts nicely with this well-structured floral arrangement. The combination keeps the arrangement from being too formal and allows it to fit easily into many different room settings.

After filling the container with floral foam and covering the foam with Spanish moss, place a row of bells-of-Ireland intermingled with pink-dyed sweet Annie across the back. Then make a row of red sweetheart roses, followed by a row of peach roses. Add a row of peach spray roses (roses with multiple blooms per stem) interspersed with small clusters of candytuft. Around the sides and front, make a skirt of German statice. Finally, add clumps of pepperberries, gluing them to the German statice if their stems are too short to insert into the foam.

DESIGN

◆

Cynthia
Gillooly

A strong contrast of horizontal and vertical elements marks this striking composition. A sheaf of oats reinforces the horizontal line of the basket, while a progression of brilliant yellow yarrow blossoms draws the eye upward. The two lines converge off center, where the spread of a pheasant wing provides a dramatic focal point.

Begin by securing a block of polystyrene foam into your container. Using a full handful of oats, wire the stems together in the center and fluff out both ends. Attach a pick to the center; then insert the pick into the foam. Now form your vertical line by adding stems of yarrow in graduated lengths. When you're happy with the overall balance, place the pheasant wing and attach it with floral pins and hot glue. Then fan the wing open, using hot glue to hold it in place. Insert two lotus pods, one in the center front and one on the right, followed by a few additional stems of yarrow. Position the eucalyptus to echo your horizontal and vertical lines; then soften the overall effect with clusters of dried bear grass picked into the top center.

DESIGN

◆

Janet Frye

Small flowers, which might appear insignificant on their own or in small clusters, take on greater importance when massed. This simple arrangement features three favorites—larkspur, annual statice, and heather—together with a few small clumps of eucalyptus berries. When making your own, be generous with the materials to assure a lush effect.

Begin by securing a block of floral foam into your container. Insert a bunch of larkspur, forming a line across the back of the base. Fan the stems slightly. Now form a second row of purple statice. Cut the statice so that the flower tops completely cover the bare stems of the larkspur but don't obscure too much of the flowers. Add a third row of heather and finish with small clusters of eucalyptus berries.

When making this arrangement, keep in mind that dried annual statice and heather are very brittle. You may find it easier to assemble the arrangement with fresh flowers and allow them to dry in place. If you do, lay the arrangement face up on a flat surface until the flowers have dried completely. This will minimize drooping stems.

DESIGN

◆

Janet Frye

This piece surely fulfills the dictum "less is more." Just three materials are used (apart from the foam and moss covering), yet the result is a dynamic composition that's fascinating to behold.

Begin with a small block of polystyrene foam covered with sheet moss. Using nine stemmed sponge mushrooms, or mushroom heads that you've picked yourself, insert the fungi into the foam in a stepped arrangement. Start at the bottom left and step each one up and to the right, keeping all of the mushrooms parallel to your work surface. Insert a bunch of dark purple larkspur into the foam; either cut the stems to a sharp point or pick small clusters to penetrate the foam. As you place the flowers, trim the height of the stems to make a torch shape. Then add a few short pieces on each side parallel to the fungi. Add a tenth sponge mushroom standing on edge at the back of the arrangement to hold the flowers steady and give it a finished appearance.

When displaying your arrangement, place three smooth, white river rocks at the base to "ground" it.

DESIGN

◆

Janet Frye

A somewhat looser structure is evident in this arrangement, where the predominant S-curve is softened by the addition of flowers and vine in the upper right to create a secondary crescent form. Wedge a block of floral foam into your container and begin placing the hydrangeas to establish a graceful, serpentine line. Use those with the shortest stems near the center of the arrangement, reserving the longer stemmed flowers for the outer edges. After making the S-curve, add a few hydrangea stems in the upper right to form a crescent. Then add honeysuckle vines to reinforce both lines.

Begin to fill in the bulk of the arrangement with sarracenia, clusters of roses, zinnias, carnations, preserved cedar, and plumosum. Although most of the flowers can be inserted directly into the foam, some of the downward-leaning pieces must first be attached to the wires, which are then inserted into the foam. Save a few roses to press well into the arrangement to give greater depth. When placing individual flowers, your goal is to create a solid mass close to the lip of the container and an airy appearance at the extremities. As a final touch, add garnishes of deep purple globe amaranth and bright yellow yarrow.

DESIGN

◆

Janet Frye

CENTERPIECES

Centerpieces can be neat and compact or tall and bushy, highly structured or loose and informal, but whatever their size and shape they must be equally attractive from every viewpoint. The fact that a centerpiece may be seen from every conceivable angle distinguishes it from a typical arrangement with a front and back. To make sure your materials are evenly distributed, turn your arrangement frequently as you assemble it.

MAKING A CENTERPIECE

DESIGN

◆

Josena McCaig

1.

Fill your container with floral foam. If your vessel is large like this one, glue two or more blocks of foam together to fill the space. Don't worry about leaving small gaps between pieces of foam.

2.

Cover the entire top surface of the foam with green sheet moss.

3.

Establish the rough outline of your arrangement by inserting pieces of greenery through the moss into the foam. This arrangement uses small clusters of sweet Annie and individual fern stems.

4.

A rule of thumb for determining a pleasing height for a centerpiece is to place your elbow on the table next to your arrangement. The height of your greenery shouldn't reach beyond the ends of your fingers. This will put the top of the arrangement just about at eye level when you're seated at the table.

5.

Place the materials that will serve as focal points in your arrangement. Here clusters of two to four stems of millet, including the grassy leaves, are picked and inserted. Other focal points include clusters of safflowers and stems of glycerine-preserved and dyed salal leaves. Brown, rather than green, floral tape is used to blend more easily with the other colors in the arrangement.

6.

Turning the container frequently as you work, fill in with individual flowers and grasses—these include sarracenia, larkspur, yarrow, roses, and rice grass. If the stems are sturdy enough, insert them directly into the foam; otherwise, pick them first.

Strive to create an even tapestry of color and texture as you add your materials. This is easier if you place all of the pieces of one material before adding the next. It also helps to take a bird's-eye view; if your arrangement is large, place it on the floor to see it from overhead.

A harmonious assortment of pinks, mauves, and greens fills this sumptuous arrangement. It's tightly packed with lots of material to make it lush when viewed from any perspective.

Secure a block of foam into your container and cover it with sheet moss. Create a low, "background" texture with clusters of German statice inserted into the foam. Then add the taller stems of pink larkspur to set the overall size of your arrangement. Turning the container frequently and adding one material at a time, fill in with annual statice, hydrangea, green amaranth, ixodia daisies, marjoram, and strawflowers. Vary the heights of your materials, setting some deep within the mass, and place them closely together. As a final accent, insert individual jade leaves in an even pattern around the arrangement.

DESIGN

◆

Jane Dicus

Variation in texture, not color, marks this stunning centerpiece. The secret to its success lies in the careful choice and placement of just a few materials—palm leaves, poppy pods, and phalaris (a type of grass).

To make a similar piece, begin by trimming five or six palm leaves into points. The naturally fan-shaped leaves can be cut with ordinary scissors, which work equally well on fresh or dried leaves. Insert the stems into a rectangular block of polystyrene foam, placing them on various levels while maintaining a strong horizontal line.

Phalaris is generally available with quite long stems. Break these roughly in half but in varying lengths. Then make clusters of 15 to 20 of the head ends, placing each cluster on a pick. Insert the picked clusters among the palm leaves on the left side of the arrangement. Repeat with the stem ends, applying them to the right side.

Apply groups of poppy pods to the top center of the arrangement by poking the stems directly into the foam. Some can be hot-glued to the palm leaves. To apply those in front, first glue a pick onto the back side of each pod; then insert the pick into the foam.

DESIGN

◆

Christopher Mello

A classic terra-cotta urn tames an arrangement of wild and woolly-looking feathers, pods, grasses, and greenery. Although it's larger in size than most tables can accommodate, this centerpiece is easily scaled down to fit your furnishings. To maintain the same look, choose materials that are about three times as long as your vase is tall.

After filling the container with floral foam, begin placing about half of the largest feathers. Arrange them in a four-sided manner, always turning the container as you work. Add the tall grasses next, with some grasses bundled together and some singly placed. As you turn the vase a quarter-turn at a time, fill in the holes with the taller stems of mini-holly, curly caustus, and preserved asparagus. Add a variety of pods, either purchased or gathered from the wild. Then intersperse the smaller greens and feathers. Make sure to save a few short feathers to insert in the center of the arrangement to give it more depth. Wherever the foam is exposed around the lip of the container, hide it with small bits of green moss hot-glued in place.

DESIGN

◆

Cathy Barnhardt

A simple gardener's trug makes an effective container for this loose, informal centerpiece that is perfect for everyday dining. There are many types of preserved greenery available; choose an assortment that shows harmony yet provides textural variation.

Secure a block of floral foam into your container and cover it with sheet moss. Placing the dried materials directly into the foam is the easiest and most natural-looking method; for a more formal approach, you may want to pick clusters of like materials.

Establish the shape of the design using bold-looking sabal palm grass and magnolia leaves. Then fill in and add interest with the varying textures, shades, and shapes of the other green materials—ivy with berries, austral fern, pimentina grass, Australian miniholly, and stems of green waxed berries. Keep the profile relatively low in the center, letting only the lightest materials add height.

Just because your space is small doesn't mean that your centerpiece should be any less grand. A graceful container—picked up at a flea market, in this case—and a carefully chosen assortment of dried flowers is all it takes.

Secure a block of floral foam into your container, allowing some of the foam to extend above the lip. This enables you to place some stems around the edges at lower angles. Establish the height of your arrangement with stems of purple marjoram and pink larkspur. Turning the container frequently, place additional larkspur and marjoram on the sides, together with white and lavender annual statice, green amaranth, and small bundles of bay leaves. Place clusters of German statice near the lip of the container so that they arc gracefully downward. Finally, add a few strawflowers and tansies for touches of color

DESIGN
◆
Jane Dicus

As perfect as a Flemish still life, this floral centerpiece makes a striking focal point for any room of the home. Its opulence comes from the generous use of air-dried peonies, which add large masses of color among the smaller, more delicate flowers.

Place a small block of floral foam into your container, leaving about 1/2 inch (1.5 cm) above the edge. If you're using a fine porcelain vase like this one, tape the foam rather than gluing it to secure it in place. Then cover the foam with sheet moss, pulling the moss gently to loosen the fibers.

Begin by establishing the height and width of the design with the pink delphinium. Cut the stems at a sharp angle and push them into the foam. Next place the larger peonies near the edge of the container and add smaller buds and rosebuds. Remember to vary the lengths of the stems and the angle of placement to give your design greater depth. Fill in with blue delphinium, Australian daisies, and blue statice. Soften the design by placing stems of springerii fern so that they cascade over the edges of the container.

DESIGN
◆
Cathy
Barnhardt

BRANCHES, VINES & DRIFTWOOD

1ichen-encrusted tree branches, gnarled and contorted vines, and hunks of sun-bleached, water-tossed driftwood make ideal frameworks for arrangements of natural materials. Whether you use them as you find them or assemble several pieces into other forms, these woody elements produce compositions that are often dramatic and always unique.

MAKING A VINE SPHERE

DESIGN

◆

Josena McCaig

1.

Assembling lengths of vine into a sphere is an easy project, and when you place two or three spheres together in an attractive bowl, they make a striking contemporary arrangement. Collect a handful of vines—grapevine or honeysuckle are most common—or purchase several ready-made miniature grapevine wreaths. These are constructed with small vines, which are more pliable than those used for larger wreaths.

2.

After cutting off the bindings and stretching out the vines, choose a section that has fewer twigs branching out of it. Form one end into a circle and secure the overlap with wire.

3.

Wrap the balance of the vine around the circle, making a second circle perpendicular to the first. Secure the two circles together with wire as needed.

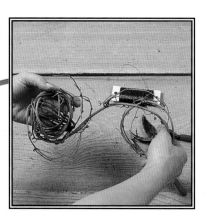

4.

Add a second vine, making an "equator" around the initial round form. Continue wrapping the vine at different angles until you begin to fill out the spherical shape. Use wire as needed to secure the ends in place.

5.

Once the sphere has been fully filled out, you can just poke the ends of the vine into it as you start and finish each new piece; securing it with wire is no longer necessary.

6.

Continue adding more vines until your sphere is as large as desired.

Building a miniature rustic chair is very easy, and the finished product makes a real conversation piece when used as a container for your floral arrangement. Select twigs of consistent thicknesses, sand the ends after cutting, and drill pilot holes before nailing them together. To embellish the basic frame, include a few vertical branches tacked across the back and a swirl of branches wired to the seat for a "cushion."

Glue a piece of sheet moss and a few sprigs of German statice onto the seat to establish a base for your flowers. First place a few taller pieces, such as small clusters of larkspur and ixodia daisies and one or two pitcher plants. Then add shorter stems of larkspur, clusters of daisies, and a few perfect roses. Fill in with hydrangea, santolina, green amaranth, and tendrils of grey-green lichen moss.

DESIGN

◆

Jane Dicus

Topiaries frequently echo the graceful form of a tree, but this arrangement is much more lifelike. With its gnarled trunk and full, windswept crown, it strongly resembles an ancient dwarfed tree growing at the peak of a mountain.

Begin building your tree with a trunk that is solid in mass and interesting in form. This one uses the remains of last year's scented geranium, but you could substitute any other sturdy annual with a good root base. After removing all of the dirt, wire the root base firmly to a fairly large rock. Camouflage the wires by gluing the roots over them and adding bits of sheet moss. If desired, enhance the trunk by gluing a few vines or gnarled branches around it. Then spray the trunk with a clear acrylic sealer.

To form the crown, clip off the top of the plant, leaving the stems about 6 inches (15 cm) long. Glue a 2-inch-thick (5-cm) block of floral foam onto the platform of stems and cover it with Spanish moss. Insert clusters of sweet Annie in various lengths to make an arc. Continue until the top is thick with sweet Annie, working the materials in the same direction to make the tree look as if it is blowing in the wind. Fill in with tansy, santolina, and billy balls. Finally, add a few sprigs of banksia leaves and curly ting-ting.

DESIGN

◆

Diane
Weaver

A rustic framework of branches and a birdhouse made of bark distinguish this eye-catching arrangement. Use gnarled branches or heavy vines, soaking them in a tub of water before bending them into the desired shape. Wire and hot-glue the pieces together as needed; then loosely weave lighter vines in the spaces where two branches are close together.

If you don't have a fallen tree from which to gather bark, construct a simple birdhouse from dark-stained plywood. Then glue on bits of dried moss and a few lichens to give it a patina. Attach the birdhouse to the framework with a liberal amount of hot glue.

Glue and wire a piece of floral foam into a suitable location on your framework. After covering the foam with sheet moss, pick several clusters of German statice and insert these into the foam to make a nearly solid covering of white. Next, begin adding individual artichokes, pomegranates, and bright yellow sunflowers or marigolds to establish the shape of the floral arrangement. Fill any gaps with Queen Anne's lace, bird-of-paradise leaves, and clusters of white berries.

Finally, glue dabs of sheet moss onto the framework for added interest.

DESIGN

◆

Bill Parker

Supple branches or heavy vines can be bent into many graceful shapes to make bases for your arrangements. In this one, a strong vine was curved into a long oval, and a couple of extra pieces were added to give the base more dimension. Wire the pieces together and cover the wires by winding lengths of honeysuckle vine over them. When shaping your branches or vines, be sure to include a place to accommodate a block of floral foam.

Wire and hot-glue the foam to the base and cover it with sheet moss. Use bits of sheet moss to cover the mechanics of your attachment. Begin inserting individual stems of the focal-point materials— Queen Anne's lace, money plant, and rye—into the foam. Angle these so that they appear to radiate outward from the center. Fill in with pink and purple larkspur, nigella, and German statice.

For a bit of whimsy, this arrangement includes two small terracotta pots glued onto one side. When attaching heavier materials such as these, be generous with the hot glue to assure a complete bond. Glue bits of sheet moss to the pots and at random places on the base to give added interest and a weathered appearance.

DESIGN
◆
Bill Parker

The demise of an established shrub isn't normally a cause for celebration, but you can reap some benefits by harvesting a few major branches for an artful dried arrangement. This one combines three pieces of an often-pruned hydrangea. The frequent clipping resulted in a profusion of small stems erupting from each main branch, which creates some interesting design possibilities.

After trimming off any extraneous wood, wire and hot-glue two or three attractive branches together. For embellishment, use stems of preserved olive to create a soft color contrast with the main wood. After determining the best placement, hot-glue the olive branches in place. Finish the composition by adding a handful of partially open pods and a few bits of lichen for accents.

DESIGN

◆

Christopher
Mello

Some of the most dramatic sculptures are created by Nature herself, when pieces of wood are worn and shaped by ocean or stream. If you don't have access to open water, explore the woods, where you'll find partially rotted stumps and roots that resemble driftwood.

Each piece of wood has a unique shape, and you can wire and glue two or more pieces together. Here a heavy piece of manzanita vine was attached to provide a strong vertical orientation, and a curlicue of kiwi vine (honeysuckle also works) was added for texture.

This piece has several ingredients native to California, but you will get similar results by substituting materials common to your own area. Two unusual eucalyptus pods look more like sea creatures than plants. Vivid touches of chartreuse are provided by letharia lichens, and brown stems of uki grass add texture. Some of the more common materials used here include pepperberries, dried mushrooms, red globe amaranths, bright yellow billy balls, viburnum berries, tallow berries, and various types of ground moss and lichen.

Any pods, berries, mosses, and lichens are suitable for driftwood arrangements. Arrange them by clustering several interesting materials to create a focal point; then work outward, adding bits of color and texture that echo your central focus. Keep in mind that the wood itself is an important element in the design; don't cover the entire surface with other materials.

DESIGN

◆

Gary Weiss

BARBARA APPLEBAUM and her husband, Lewis, own and operate Brush Creek Gardens in Fairview, North Carolina. They grow 200 varieties of organic herbs and flowers, which they air dry. Barbara was formerly an art teacher and florist, and she now enjoys making custom-designed arrangements.

■

CATHY BARNHARDT is in charge of the floral department at Biltmore House in Asheville, North Carolina, the largest private home in North America. Her specialty is working with texture and depth, and she enjoys composing dramatic pieces in a single color to emphasize both.

■

ANNE COOK is a Welsh-born designer who developed her skills in floral arts at Biltmore House. For nine years she has designed and created floral arrangements displayed throughout the estate. Anne's sumptuous designs reflect the English garden style and often include a touch of whimsy.

JANE DICUS owns Dutch Cove Herbs and Everlastings in Winston-Salem, North Carolina. In addition to being a full-time teacher, she dries her own locally grown ingredients and designs and executes all of her floral arrangements, which she markets at craft fairs throughout the eastern United States.

■

JANET FRYE is the owner of The Enchanted Florist in Arden, North Carolina, where she indulges her passion for creating innovative designs with natural materials. She has had her own business for a decade and has applied her creative touch to floral design for 18 years.

■

CYNTHIA GILLOOLY and JAMIE MCCABE often collaborate to create their distinctive floral arrangements. Cynthia owns The Golden Cricket, a floral design studio in Asheville, North Carolina, where she also teaches classes. Jamie, a fellow designer in the shop, enjoys including a few uncommon materials in her arrangements. Together they have more than 25 years of floral design experience.

PATTI HILL lives at Mountain Shadows Farm in Weaverville, North Carolina, where she gathers most of the materials for her natural arrangements from the nearby woods. In addition to creating wreaths and other designs, Patti is a weaver and basket artist, and she makes beaded jewelry.

■

JOSENA AIELLO MCCAIG operates her own floral design studio called Some Parlor Ivy in Asheville, North Carolina. Josena polished her design skills while working as a floral display artist at Biltmore House. Dried flowers are her passion, and she loves to combine them in large masses to create lush designs.

■

CHRISTOPHER MELLO is a horticulturist who comes to floral design through the garden. Above all else he loves gardening and collecting natural materials from the woods surrounding his home in Marshall, North Carolina. He practices his art as a floral designer at Biltmore House.

BILL PARKER and his wife, Nan, own Parker Patch Crafts in Mountain Rest, South Carolina. Bill was a professional florist for 10 years and now collaborates with his wife to make specialty handcrafts. He is a "natural" at floral design and usually works by letting his materials guide his compositions.

■

DIANE WEAVER and her husband, Dick, own Gourmet Gardens, an herb nursery and specialty shop located in Weaverville, North Carolina. Diane dries many of the more than 180 varieties of herbs they grow, and she uses them to create distinctive natural arrangements and herbal condiments.

■

GARY WEISS owns and operates Ixia, a floral design studio in San Francisco, California. His work is strongly influenced by Asian and European designs and reflects his attention to small details. Gary's favorite arrangements are sculptural pieces that include a variety of mosses and unusual pods.

Heartfelt thanks are extended to all of the talented floral designers and to Dana Irwin, my art director and partner in this project. Their boundless creativity and artistry are responsible for making this book more beautiful in every way.

The hospitality of those who opened their homes to our camera—Ivo Ballentine and Robin Cape, Faye and Carter Brown, Jean Chesnutt, Joan Lonnes, and Susan Roderick—is gratefully acknowledged. Thanks also to those who allowed us to photograph some beautiful settings at their places of business: Roanne Bishop at the Johnson Farm in Hendersonville, North Carolina; Jean Brooks at Pine Crest Inn in Tryon, North Carolina; David Bruce at Camp Rockmont in Black Mountain, North Carolina; Theo, Mark, and Ted Kerhulas at The Tea House in Tryon, North Carolina; and Ann Whisenhunt at In-The-Oaks Episcopal Conference Center in Black Mountain, North Carolina.

Special thanks go to Ivo Ballentine at Preservation Hall in Asheville, North Carolina, who was unfailing in his generosity and capacity to produce the perfect prop. For their assistance with photography, thanks also to Linda Constable at Sluder Furniture, Shelly Jones and Michael Murphy at Preservation Hall, and Diane Weaver.